White Rose Bards

2022

Edited by
James P. Wagner (Ishwa)

Table of Contents

M. M. Barton

Liquid Silk

My affection for you is liquid silk dripping on my skin.
Your love for me seeps through the cracks of decades old lost wins.

We watch the diamonds in the sky, such fragile, pin pricked things.
I long to chase moonlight with you until I die, and we fly away on frost-kissed paper wings.

My delight in you is morning mist, chasing my weather weary soul.
You see something shine within me, and I bite my lip, for fear the sensation may swallow me whole.

I want to be consumed by you.
Hungrily smothered.
Devoured from inside out.
Your wolf-strong arms around my feather boned shoulders.
I'd spend life happily like that, without a doubt.

I'd like to be enveloped by you.
Your kisses capturing me in one fell swoop, our heartbeats fluttering within ribcages coated with gold.
This liquid silk upon my skin will never again turn cold.

M. M. Barton is a writer, actress, and singer raised in the historic city of York. When she's not walking her dog or working on recording music with her father, she can be found typing in a word document so furiously it's a wonder her keyboard is still in one piece, making lavender bags on her sewing machine, or curled up under a blanket watching a true crime documentary. Having written since she could hold a pen, M. M. Barton has been crafting escapist worlds for herself in the form of writing since she can remember. When mental health or life gets her down, writing is the sure fire way to bring her back up once more.

Janet Beadle

Pied Piper

I'm told, by those who saw it
his car crawled quietly in to town,
slithered to a stop, unremarked.

I'm told he sidled to the square
where our children played heedlessly
intent on hide and seek, follow my leader.

I'm told he opened his netted bag
and offered his apple-dab sweeties-
the youngest first, little Tamara.

I'm told she was doubtful, memory-bells pealing
then, tasting the tangy sweet pleasure
she called Anastasia and my gentle Natalya.

I'm told he lured them to his car
gently, promising them a short, pretty ride.
Girls chosen, for once, before boys.

I'm told the door closed with a hiss
before the car snaked softly away
out of our village, out of our sight, out of our reach.

I'm told the girls can now be viewed in celluloid form
in any foreign city or far-off land,
men's performing puppet playthings.

Tamara, Anastasia, my own lovely Natalya.

Janet was born in Beverley, grew up in Holderness, before attending school in York. She worked in the East End of London for many years before being ordained in York Minster. She is now retired from parish ministry and lives again in York.

Ruth Bellass

In Ephemeral Pink

Broken by the spring rain,
these fleeting blooms
cannot hold.

Released to the breeze,
briefly borne,
to live for a moment
then fade and fall.

Jaded dreams
crushed flat
like transient pink.

I cling to them,
but my grasp is weak,
for all things pass
as they slip in time.

And what is left after the storm,
but a carpet of wet petals.

Soon a memory,
swept away.

Ruth is East Riding born and bred. She started writing in the first Lockdown when words came to fill the empty days.

Thomas Binns

It's been a while since I've seen you smile

It's been a while, since I've seen you smile,
The cursed human race.
It's been a while, since I've seen your smile
A mask still covers your face.
Do you still rejoice, join together in voice
To sing, celebrate and dance?
Do you still rejoice, join together in voice
Or has the screen got you in a trance?
Do you look at the other, as if he's your brother
And meet them eye to eye?
Do you look at the other, as if she's your mother
Or are you afraid to even say hi?
Do you feel the emotion, above all the commotion
Or are you drowning in despair?
Do you feel the emotion, above all the commotion?
Show your neighbour that you care
It's been a while, since I've seen you smile
And the news is full of fear.
It's been a while, since I've seen your smile
Which once was ear to ear.

Mr Thomas was born in Bradford, studied education in York and has family throughout all parts of Yorkshire. He has lived and taught in Africa, Italy and Asia, but always returns home to God's Own County. The poems selected for this anthology were written whilst living in York in 2021

Rebecca Bostock

Queen Bee

You are infinitely gracious,
Delightful and courageous.
Most are entranced,
by your utterly fascinating waggle-dance.

For you have incomparable charm,
so this is not by chance,
Under your guide the hive will come to no harm.
All that look up to thee are likely to be filled with glee,
The gem of your colony.

Your kindness and compassion knows no boundaries,
Highly respected.
So ferociously protected by your offspring,
You have the capacity to sting and sting,
Any rival wanna be queens,
this is how you reign supreme.

The workers are eternally in your debt,
Grateful for the love you show to the hive.
Thus ensuring,
the Bostock colony is bound to thrive

Rebecca Bostock (Bex) is a 40 year old Bradford lass who in 2017 discovered her enjoyment of poetry through a friend whom she met via activism. The following year she started writing her own poems.

Stef Bricklebank

Behind the locked door

What did you fear behind the locked door?
What did you imagine would happen?
If the door became unlocked?
What did you fear?

Behind the locked door
The purposely locked door
You chose to lock the door
You chose to bolt the door
At what point did you make that decision?

Behind the locked door
Did you feel safe?
Did you feel secure?
Did you settle in to a great nights sleep?
Or did you lay awake in fear?
On tenterhooks listening out for every noise?
Waiting to for him to stand the other side of the locked door?

Behind the locked door
Who's idea was it?
Why was it there?
Many explanations were given
But all were pretend.

Behind the locked door
I hope you felt safe from whatever you feared
I hope you felt calm
I hope you slept peacefully
I hope you felt safe
Behind the locked door

Do you still use the locked door?
It's still there the lock
Still there, in all it's glory
As a reminder of the past?
Or do you still feel the fear and need the locked door?

Stef Bricklebank lives in York, North Yorkshire and is best known for her honest and raw written word. A lover of words and self expression, Stef is a poet, educator and confidence consultant. Let her take you on a journey. You can chat with Stef on Instagram at @stefbricklebank or check out her website at www.stefbricklebank.com 'Behind The Locked Door' was written in September 2020.

Paul Brooks

A Belated Prayer

My mother simply evaporated
I could not speak or feel related.
It all came as a surprise
death beheld those sorry eyes.
An ageing body was took away
In the silence of that day.
I never kissed to say goodbye
or find Jesus as he walked by.
It was the breaking of the bread
That took the pain from her head.

Paul was born in York UK. He loved the arts, poetry, philosophy and animals. Paul had to cope with significant mental and physical health challenges. He found solace in poetry and art. He died on March 27th 2022 so he never knew his poem was published.

Matthew Clare

I Wish I'd Known

A cold wind howls through the night,
Like wolves turning to the moon,
But I am spent and cannot fight,
And sit trapped by my own gloom.

Scared and alone, I do nought but think,
As I try to peer through my foggy haze,
Only to be edged closer to the brink.
My sorry existence, an insufferable maze.

I look about and around, up and down.
Noone to break my silence.
I breathe, close eyes, and smooth my frown,
I lean forward and throw off my balance.

The wind should rush by me.
The sound should deafen my ears.
There is nought but tranquillity,
A calm unrivalled in years.

My eyes open slowly and I start to see,
Everything I've wanted, the answers to all,
The things to choose, the things I could be,
Were I not now mid-fall.

The calm betrays me, a panic does start,
As I try to reverse my descent.
A rage, a despair, a pain all fill my heart,
As I focus on the approaching cement.

Now I can feel the wind,
Pushing against me, willing me to go back.
Starting to hope for some angel's wings,
To save me from the ground's attack.

There is nothing to delay my plight.
I wince as I try to fight gravity's pull,
Wishing I'd known I had more fight,
Or that I'd lived my life more full.

But no. Options are spent.
What's done is done.
A fate I cannot circumvent,
As I approach the end of my run.

I'm well beyond the mid-point now.
Wishing I could take this back.
Wishing my jump, I could disavow.
Wishing I was not soaring into the eternal black.

I look to the top, high above,
Hoping upon hope that I get back there,
With the life I chose to dispose of,
As I close off a feeble and pitiful prayer.

The ground approaches again,

Like a friend, ready to embrace.
I tremble in fear at the nearing terrain,
My missteps, I wish there were time to replace.

I close my eyes.
I give up and wait for it.
I should have said more goodbyes,
I should have done so much more before this hit.

This is the end now.
A second or two left not much.
My mind refuses silence somehow,
And continues to struggle, to avoid death's touch.

Final thoughts before my smite,
One and one only does my attention pull:
"I wish I'd known I had more fight,
And that I'd lived my life more full".

Matthew Peter Clare, a musician and writer living and working in York. I principally work in the theatre; however, have turned my hand towards poetry as a way of expressing some of my less enjoyable life moments in a healthier way than I may have done so in the past.

Peter J Donnelly

The White Horse of Kilburn

Not calved in chalk hillside
like its southern cousins
by which it was inspired,
but sandstone. An illusion,
though not as you'd think.
Motorists on the A1 were not fooled,
nor passengers in trains to Scotland
and the North. It could have stayed
a grey stallion or beige mare,
but instead must be covered
with limestone from the distant Wolds
from where you can see it
on clear days. The work of a local
businessman and a schoolmaster,
did they imagine how hard
it would be to whitewash or paint,
that it would have to be hidden
in wartime, masked from German bombers?

We walk to its head
not to admire it, but rather the view
from the bench at the top of
the steps, strangely not spoilt
by power station chimneys.
In summer we may

pick bilberries along the way.
There are always gliders,
once a display of birds of prey,
and very often people we know.

Peter J Donnelly lives in York where he works as a hospital secretary. He has a degree in English Literature and a MA in Creative Writing from the University of Wales Lampeter. He has been published in various magazines and anthologies including York Literary Review. He recently won second prize in the Ripon Poetry Festival competition.

Kevin Flaherty

Cloth Cap Rap

Have you heard the latest thing going down
Sung by the oldest swinger in town?
It's the cloth cap rap, the cloth cap rap.
Snapping my fingers, keeping in time
Chanting the words to the rhythm and rhyme
Dunno know if it's rap, dunno know if it's hip-hop
It goes on non-stop; I never stay in one spot
No problem now since my long-awaited hip op.
All the oldies listening tell me that it's tip top
All the young ones thinking that I sound like a crackpot
Wearing my cloth cap, pulling on my tank top
Bouncing round in flip flops, dancing the foxtrot
Cruising in my soft-top, I wipe away a dewdrop
Looking like a sexpot, searching for a hotspot
Warming up my tea pot, I call at the chip shop.
So I'm sitting with my coat on, the heating's off, it's getting cold
I'm starting with a bad cough, looking rough or so I'm told
I've got my scarf and gloves, on you feel it when you're getting old
Watching the TV, drinking my cocoa
You know it makes me want to pee, it's always a no-no.
I wander off and into town, wearing my dressing gown
It's the highlight of the week and I'm feeling the tension
Queuing at the Post Office, picking up my pension
Life is good, well, on the whole
Sex and drugs and sausage rolls.

19

So I'm sucking on a polo, acting like a renegade
I'm tired of going solo, I need someone to serenade
Looking for adventure, out with the lasses
Fixing my dentures, cleaning my glasses
Chatting up a barmaid, adjusting my hearing aid
She's putting up a barricade, she's not that easy to persuade.
I took a coach trip to the Lakes, bought some Kendal mint cake
Fed the ducks, stayed awake, had a toasted teacake
Tea and scone, slice of cake, Gaviscon, bellyache.
The driver's looking irate, he's getting in a right state
"Get back on t' coach for Pete's sake,
Every time we come up here there's allus one that makes us late."
So I'm standing in the library, reading the tabloids
I tell the librarian "I'm suffering with haemorrhoids"
here's what she says to me "Call at the Pharmacy"
I think I'll go to A&E; I'll get the ointment there for free.
I'm flirting with the piles nurse, she tells me they're getting worse.
I want to ask her for a date, she said she needs to concentrate
"I'm pulling on the glove mate,
lift up the gown and bend down
I need to check your Prostate".
It's the cloth cap rap, the cloth cap rap.
Well, I've snapped my fingers and I've kept in time
I've chanted the words to the rhythm and rhyme
I've ranted and raved, I'm no longer in my prime
With one foot in the grave I'm on borrowed time
I'm feeling my age and it's way past my bed time.

Kevin Flaherty has been writing and performing poetry for over 20 years. He is a slam winner, has won a number of poetry competitions and has been published in various anthologies. His poetry covers a wide range of topics but with an emphasis on humour and dialect.

Siobhan Gifford

Phantom block

I stubbed my toe against a writer's block
squatting like a fat cat in the hallway
of my famined mind, spine arched, ginger rock,
a siege against my reach for lyric sway
and beat. On its flanks, scars of bardish names
etched in pentameter far beyond my
skill, hissing assonance and mewling blame
for wayward metaphors I misapply.

Nouns pound against the pulsing ground below
my feet; similes flail to be set free
to sneer like birds in telegraphic rows,
black quaver crows, unfinished symphony.

And then...*and then*...words cartwheel into line.
As phantom block cavorts to reeling rhyme.

Siobhan Gifford lives in a village a few miles north of the wonderful medieval city of York where she loves the puzzle of grasping an image, an action, an emotion and a glimpse of the astonishing North Yorkshire scenery to create a jigsaw of memory.

Kitty Greenbrown

The Long Weekend

We woke to snow in the unknown valley
Everything labelled Holiday-Only

Your Step Mum threw up her April hands when it was all over and
done
This deep, this long after Easter?
Our Emma, she'll not get past Ripponden

My smile is weak as tea
Feet made fat by wet boots
Good leather lasagned by the four mile hike in calf deep snow
With two crying children in tow

More gravy love?
Cheeks burn coldly by the gas fire
I shake my head
How did you end up walking into Hebden then?

Can I give you lift? He said
Blue pick-up truck the only living thing in the thorough white
There won't be any buses, the valley's blocked
I had to check the flock up top
Where are you going with the kids in this snow?
You're all soaked through
Tubs of sheep feed lugged across

We pack three to the front seat, smallest on my knee

So what's the story? Or maybe I shouldn't ask?
I won't be able to get you right to town love
But I can get you as near as

I put one small hand in each of mine
Windscreen wipers bat fresh flakes to either side
Mum how far is it? Not too far I lie
I set my jaw for town like a sat nav
I can carry you one at a time on my back
That's the best I can do, I say

Nothing's open, but there's a light on in Age UK
She looks up, stands up, Glenys get towels love
And put the kettle on
See if there are leggings for the little ones - and socks
No, don't worry about the floor love, we can mop.
How far have you come? Cragg Vale? You never!
Well, at least it's stopping
Not exactly, I think. He has his own weather.

Kitty Greenbrown is a performance poet with a keen interest in telling stories. She's a Say Owt Slam and York Culture Awards winner, and has supported both Kate Fox and Hollie McNish live. Recent projects include live poetry for the Bloomsbury Group exhibition at York Art Gallery, a poetry in the landscape commission for North York Moors National Park and a highly commended poem in The Poetry Archive's World View competition, judged by Simon Armitage and Imtiaz Dharker.

Libby Greenhill

A Sense of Winter

Look out of the window,
See the white,
The blanket that smothers the grass.
Look at the blue
That encases the trees,
Look at that dripping ice.
See the cool blue of frosty sky,
The freezing shards of sun.
Wait for a second, just look- a twittering robin,
See that red as it blends-brown.
See honour planted on face.

Now open the door, step into the wild.
Feel that crunch of the cold snow on your feet.
Put your hand on a tree,
Feel ice liquefy,
Seep into your hand.
Stop for a second as your hand becomes cold- heart grows warm.
Close your eyes,
Feel the wind on your eye lids,
Take a deep breath of air,
Feel a cold rush in your throat.
The frost in the air crisp on your skin,
Feel this winter wonderland surround you.

Open your eyes,
Hold a hand to ear-
Hear the song,
Birds beautiful twitter.
Listen intently to harmony,
Delight in winter tunes.
Take a step forward,
Hear that crunch,
The melody of snow.
Close your eyes and just listen,
Listen to the wind, as it wraps the trees, keeps them secure,
and whistles along to winter song.

Take a breath through your nose,
Take in atmosphere.
Smell the ice as it waves through air,
Smell bark of trees as they linger in your nostrils.
Take another deep breath,
Feel the scents of frost as they seep into mind,
Freeze you into winter bliss.

Now,
Before you leave this glowing world,
Just taste the air as it fills your lungs,
Just taste that chestnut from tree.
Just taste the sunbeams rain down on earth,
Splitting into shards,
Filling you with worth.
Feel taste of melting snow.

Taste winter at its fullest,
The fragrance of leaves in air fills throat
With taste of silence, peace.

Libby Greenhill is a home educated thirteen year old from York, who is passionate about writing, especially poetry and creative writing. She had her first book published when she was seven and has been writing ever since. She hopes to study creative writing in university and one day pursue it as a career.

Oz Hardwick

Pluck

Yesterday's storm blew down the bunting we'd hung to welcome the soldiers home. It blew down the trees we'd planted to welcome the parakeets home, and it blew down the notional barriers we'd erected between our good old days and our brave new world. So, when the heroes came marching down that long, dusty road, whistling music hall tunes to fill in the spaces left by missing limbs and repressed trauma, we were too busy with the birds to notice. When they'd left they'd weighed 63 grams, but when they returned they were 2 ¼ ounces and their passports had changed from red to blue. Civil servants, wrapped in red tape and fluttering bunting, flailed rubber stamps like inky windmills as snapping beaks demanded crackers and demanded to know who exactly was a pretty boy, while stiff troops, sweating as they shouldered pikes and nuclear warheads, grew dusty in the town square. Yesterday's storm blew down the back streets and boulevards, sweeping feathers to who knows where. Now, the market sellers are setting out their stalls, pricing in shillings and pence, while children crowd round black and white TVs to watch grey parakeets migrating in leaky dinghies. Yesterday's storm blew down soldiers like skittles, so who's going to drive the lorries now?

Oz Hardwick is a European prose poet, whose work has been widely published in international journals and anthologies. His tenth collection, *A Census of Preconceptions*, will be published by SurVision Books in 2022. Oz is Professor of Creative Writing at Leeds Trinity University. www.ozhardwick.co.uk

Richard Harries

Spanish Flu

Written in lockdown 2020

World War 1 has always moved
And fascinated me
A vast tragedy on such a huge scale
Families and communities decimated
A generation of young men annihilated
Whenever I read or studied about it
I often saw that afterwards many were killed
By the Spanish Flu
Did not register greatly
Not full of action and trenches
No Mans Land and blood

It was a pandemic

50 million died
50 million who had just been bereaved
50 million isolated and confused

No TV or radio to inform them
No call boxes
Phones were only for the rich
No Community hubs, mobile phones
Google, computers

Just terror and illness and death

Having lived through the strain of this pandemic
I wonder at their strength to survive at all
I am horrified for them
And ashamed I did not comprehend what they went through

Richard Harries is a poet approaching 70 years of age. He has one Anthology published by Stairwell books of York and another on its way in October 2022 ICONIC TATTOO. He has appeared on Zoom during the pandemic all over the world . He has lived in North , West and East Yorkshire all his life. In normal times he appears all over the North of England at festivals and charity events.

Angela Harrison

The Yorkshire Troubadour

I searched for a trace of the musical gene
That set my life course into motion.
It didn't take long to uncover a scene
Of which I'd had little notion.

My grandmother's granddad, in days of yore,
Well, he'd caught scarlatina so young.
Poor Richard was feverish, his rash was quite sore
Couldn't feed for the lumps on his tongue.

But worse was to come, complications so cruel
which stripped the poor lad of his sight.
His parents in shock, quickly found him a school -
an asylum for boys in his plight.

He learnt pretty well, as best that he could,
in those days there was little on offer.
Weaving small baskets, working with wood -
any tasks that the tutors could proffer.

One day when the vicar had played them a psalm,
He asked our young boy to recite it.
But no, with a strong voice he sang it, so calm
although inside he felt quite excited.

This was the start of the great things to come
through the Brighton/York Blind School connection
He learnt fiddle and on the school's harp he would strum
skills uncovered by one brief infection.

He went back to Kent when he reached a good age
Father gone, his mother'd remarried.
It didn't seem right to be there, at that stage
There was nothing to gain if he tarried.

Richard fell for a woman who'd stayed by his side,
up to Yorkshire they went with an infant.
Five more children were born (although two of them died)
one musician - they knew in an instant.

Father and son proved a popular act
using violins, harp and the voice.
In Dewsbury, Ossett and Pontefract
Their duo was always first choice.

Alas, Richard's son died - not 30 years old,
and 'Blind Dick' as he'd come to be known
fell into a sadness, or so it is told
And began to sing songs of his own.

He sang of his childhood, his love and his fear
He sang of being different - being blind
He sang of his hopes for his children so dear
His words were quite gentle and kind.

"Ee Dick", they would say, "your songs are so sweet
We'll book you to sing us some more.
These musical talents – they cannot be beat
You're a fine Yorkshire Troubadour!"

Dick passed on the gene to his daughter and then
To *her* daughter, who taught me to play.
So, I finally know the line of descent, when
I thank my good fortune each day.

Angela Harrison has enjoyed two careers - one as a professional viola
player, the other as a Music Therapist. Born in Leeds, she is
fascinated by the lives of her forebears and writes prose and poetry
as a legacy for those who follow. Angela now lives on a farm in North
Yorkshire and increasingly spends her time playing chamber music
with friends.

Tatty Hoggarth

Too Many Shark Movies

I thought I'd seen them all, but there must've been one I missed
I thought as I pulled out a copy of Shark Exorcist
Piles upon piles of films all about a shark
There's so many of these things, they've certainly left their mark

I found Sharknado and Deep Blue Sea
Robo Shark, Jurassic Shark and Jaws 3D!

How have they made so many, how has this come to be?
Why can't so many people just stay out of the bloody sea!?!
Or at least that's what I thought, untill I went and bought
Creature where the shark is a land walking juggernaut

I saw so many shark films and soon I did discover
That most of the budget was spent on doing the front cover
I thought I'd watch something different with a classic story arc
Bit I accidentally picked up Raiders of The Lost Shark!

It ruined my weekend, all of my money spent
On accidentally picking up this great white accident
There's a lesson that I learnt, I'll pass it on to you
You'd never live near the bloody sea if any of these films were true!

Tatty Hoggarth is a ranting punk poet from Bradford, West York-
shire. He is the resident poet of the 1in12 club and has been perform-
ing poetry for over 10 years.

Kim Hosking

Entwined

Lying in the back of his pickup truck,
Friends unaware in the front,
I'm as quiet as a mouse,
As silent as the grave,
Heart hammering,
Sneaking, creeping, loving, wanting,
All of it entwined.

Climbing out your bedroom window
As the front door closes,
As wild as electricity,
As alive as I can be,
Breath racing,
Power, sex, remorse, guilt,
All of it entwined.

Holding onto this secret,
Praying no one can see,
As dark as the night,
But clear as daylight,
Ache deepening,
Lies, promises, scandal, words,
Begging to be caught.

Kim is an archaeologist by day, and a writer whenever the muse strikes; when not in a muddy trench she can be found wrapped, burrito-style in a blanket, a book and brew in hand. She longs for the day magic, or science, will give us dragons and she can take to the skies…

Maggie Jackson

A Hunslet Peace

Being ground down by dereliction,
one day I cleared a patch of soil
and planted bright begonias
to bring some colour to my battered door,
hoping to bejewel a dismal street.

Next day I found the brightness darkened,
the plants uprooted and left to die.
Rage spread like poison to my green fingers,
my gentle gardening nature found a killer instinct,
keen to spray with pesticide the unknown enemy
who had wantonly ruined my oasis of hope.

And then, a multi-coloured movement caught my eye:
a child, vibrant as the flowers of her distant homeland,
crouched in a patch of sunlight,
pouring water from a plastic cup
onto a begonia she had newly planted,
her trowel a lollipop stick with which she scraped the earth,
wisely creating a garden that would not wither for want of sun.

Having no language we could share,
we wordlessly dug and watered;
moving anger from its mulch of darkness,
changing judgment into fertile kindness,

soaking the soil with tears of forgiveness,
grafting joy onto a Hunslet terrace,
and rooting peace between two Hunslet hearts.

Maggie Jackson lives in Selby (North Yorkshire) where she writes poetry, short stories, vignettes, satirical and contemplative reflections. She has published poetry in several anthologies, journals and on websites. Her collection "Offertory: poems from a monastery" was the product of being a Poet in Residence in 2017 in Mirfield, West Yorkshire.

Richard Jenkins

Sell the House

Sell the house sell the car sell your will
I did not agree to have my keyboard quill
Perverted by a petty shrivelling
Not willing
To have you win out to the last
Your ruin was brought in a bargain basement blast
Woolworths for the woolheaded
Time your shedded the skin
Of scaly illusion
And my collusion
Has prevented its dilution
The dreams you surrender
Were not yours to sell,
Or squander.

Karen Leaf

84 Days In Lockdown

(written when the government announced that shops were open again....and what that did to us!!)

Cupboards are clean,
Lawns are cut
Dead headings done,
The gate is shut

Nobody visits
I'm knitting a scarf
I've jet washed the path
I'm clapping NHS staff

I would've been in the shops
I would've been meeting friends
I would've been seen the hairdresser
Got rid of my split ends

But no – I baked my 10th cake
I've learnt to play drums
I'm doing on "on line" exercise class
for legs bums and tums

I've painted my finger nails
Done the face masks
I'm sat with a puzzle

but there's no-one here to ask

But today somethings happening
There's something to do
The shops have opened
So I can stand in the queue!!

Day 84 and I can leave the house
But first I need to find
"proper clothes" to wear
I seem to have left them behind

Loungewear, leggings baggy jumpers
No make-up and comfy clothes
Has become the norm for me
I'm taking off my slippers but look at my toes

I'm reaching for my skirt
But it just doesn't fit
But those cookery programmes
Were too good to miss

My shoes are so uncomfortable
My poor feet hurt
And I can't fasten the buttons
Anymore on this shirt

This is impossible
My clothes just don't fit
Take a deep breath

And push and pull
With that zip

Right, I'm dressed and now
The difficulty starts
Putting make up on for the first time
Is really quite an art

It's the same routine I used before
Same colours, concealer "my clay"
But I can't apply it that well, because
I can't see cos my fringe is in the way

Oh my hair, the colour, the length
The straight bits, the waves,
the thickness, the locks
The roots, the greys

I look in the mirror
I see this person looking back
I ask it
Do you think I'd look better in a sack.

I find the bag, the car keys
And a shopping list or two
I went to this bother
To stand in a queue!

Karen Leaf has been writing poems just for fun for more years than she can remember. She enjoys the story telling, the challenges of capturing a moment, creating a rhythm and being playful with words. Karen has never entered a competition in her life and decided that needed to change. She has a notepad and pen everywhere she goes because there is always something to capture or observe. Poetry is there to be written, ready and enjoyed. Its Karen's best friend!

Rachel Lister- Jones

The Restless Soul

Your soul crashes through the house
Angrily banging doors
And rattling windows.
You wanted to live forever
And now you're dead.
Your soul is restless,
It doesn't know what to do with itself.
Tired and fretful I try to reassure it,
"Hold on Dad, I'll let you out," I say,
Frantically opening windows,
Wide open, despite the rain,
"I'll let you go back to Mum,"
But your soul can't go, won't go
This is your house,
You have lived here for more than forty years,
You're a respected member of the community.
Why should you go?
I leave you to it.
I walk along childhood's familiar paths
Through wood, field, town,
Over packhorse bridge
Along the trout-brown river
Past elegant Georgian facades
And post-war semis.
I walk for hours.

I am restless too.
I don't want you to go, but you must.
Your soul cannot stay here
Where it loves,
It must go to those it loves
Who went before it.
It belongs with the dead
Not the living.
When I get home you're still there
Quieter but still present.
My brother phones.
He pleads with me to go to his house.
He is restless too.
"I am going to Simon's," I shout to Dad,
As I did when I went out as a teenager
All those years ago,
"We love you Dad but you must go
This is not where you belong now,"
I leave the house again
And drive past your old haunts
Where you were born
Eighty odd years ago
Your life has been long
But not long enough
You've done a lot
And now there's no time for more.
Simon asks how I am,
I cry and say, "He won't go,
He needs to be with Mum,
But he doesn't want to miss Christmas."
When I arrive home

-Although soon it will no longer be that-
I cautiously put the worn key in the lock
And open the door.
Something has changed.
There is no more crashing,
No more presence.
You have flown,
Like the birds you loved,
To a better place.
All is quiet,
All is still,
You are free.

Rachel Lister-Jones is born and bred in North Yorkshire and now lives in Easingwold with her whippet, Lady Millicent. She has written since she was a child but only started writing poetry six years ago after her father died. She is inspired by the natural world and her poems explore the themes of grief, memory, and the connection with the natural world.

Maria Grazia Lucrezia Leotta

The Dales' Dream

I walked alone in the silence of my inner thoughts
and touched the ancient castle's walls.
I heard the sound of my own footsteps
echoing in the shadow of the Prince's Tower.

Laughs, voices, joy and grief,
a child's wooden sword,
hooves on pebbles,
rosemary and lily,
grass and rose.
The North wind blew
pushing away the clouds that covered the waving Dales
under the cobalt sky
of Middleham's cold winter.

I heard horses and armours,
men's steps on the ground,
women screaming in the pain of giving life,
and an old love song played on lute and shawm
lost in centuries, found in memories that arise now.
High and proud sparkled the beacon's flame
the resounding horns of excited hunters.

"Welcome" said the Lord of the North,
"Welcome to my castle of dreams"

as he offered me a golden goblet
of mead and madeira
at the table of honour from which we surveyed a raucous party
on the twelfth day of Christmas.
Red faces burning for the wine
under a carved stone mantelpiece
heat radiated from the bright hearth
as the fire consumed the logs with its greedy flames.

A crown and an ermine robe,
a tabard of murrey and blue
the throne's supreme glory,
the heartbreaking death
of England's rightful heir
the river Ure sang a lament of mourning for the true king.

I walked alone in the silence of my inner thoughts
under the gloomy sky
of Middleham's cold winter
and touching the ancient castle's walls
it was there I found my soul.

Maria Grazia Lucrezia Leotta was born in Italy and graduated in Modern Foreign Languages and Literature. Nine years ago, thanks to a bursary from the University of Sheffield, she moved to England with her family and she took an MA Translation Studies. She fell in love with York and in 2019 she moved there. She is an interpreter and translator, the Secretary of the Scottish Branch of the Richard III Society and a researcher for The Missing Princes Project for Philippa Langley who successfully led the search to locate King Richard III grave.

Syeda Rumana Mehdi

One-Sided Love

The weak smell
Of rose petals
Put lovingly between
Pages of a thick book

Pen struts across the page
Pausing here and there
Looking at me mockingly

Dresses are worn
Only to be discarded
In a pile on my bed

Tears flow freely
Sometimes landing on the carpet
Like soft raindrops
Sometimes pausing on my cheeks
Like a caress
Sometimes spreading like blots
Across my chiffon shirt

I twirl around my room
The mirrors shows a lonely girl
Outside, autumn leaves fall silently
What do you know
About the pain of one-sided love?

Syeda Rumana Mehdi is a recent graduate in Women and Gender Studies from University of York and is currently pursuing her passion of teaching literature from a feminist perspective. She is currently exploring politics of translation and identity in her poetry and enjoys to cook and crochet in her free time.

Ella Potter

Familiar Streets

A welcome stranger wanders through my door
of my past etched on celluloid films

A mat woven with the mud of countless shoes
Welcomes me into a clock that etched away my time

Lonely swings and broken roundabouts
Once alive with innocent minds

Hopscotch rhymes twinkle
Carefree love echoes the joy of beauty

As chaotic stones clink at the mercy of chance
A bounty of woodland hides safe in a pocket

Birds swoop with camera-flash confidence
A summer flower immune to winter chills

The play of lights on feral streets
Illuminate footfalls kissing the ground

Such intense infusion of rose-budded parks
To go back and relive childhood romance

Ella Potter is a 20-year-old poet from Harrogate, North Yorkshire, and has an interest in nostalgic, landscape, and romantic poetry. She studies Creative Writing and English Literature at Edge Hill University and is a runner-up in the Liverpool Poetry Prize, hosted by Roger McGough.

Tahira Rehman

Mirage

Chasing the mirage
like a fool
but it's too cool
for my hands to stay away

it's too sweet, almost like a treat
once in a while.
but when the sun goes down,
there is only darkness -
darker than my eyes when they are closed,
darker than a seceret that is not exposed.

How naïve I am to take you to the heights I do
Without closing my eyes I dream about you
I dream of greenery reaching the stars
I dream of it coming true
No more broken memories
No more scars
I taste a sweetness
of the past
except is it real?
will I fail
again to see
the reality

the mind is like crossed pathways
giving way to every thought
yet it collides together
like never ending congestion
there are no empty spaces in between
or ends to the road

just continues rocky hills
that never seem to end
I despise my own self
Yet I appreciate my feelings
they are mine

Tahira Rehman is a Performance-Poet and an Outreach support worker in Leeds. She has headlined at festivals and events such as Spoken Weird, Punk in Drublic, Cellar Stories at the Lawrence Batley theatre and she has supported a touring show at the Gosforth Civic Theatre.

Annisa Suliman

Auction Shed

The cattle market auction shed is haven,
a muffin of breeze blocks and corrugated iron.
For city folk caught in summer storms
this drama is pastoral idyll.
Yet the serenity is drenched in desperation,
ghosts of countless herds parade the inner whorl;

Off the walls and roof waves
soldiers' voices ricochet

hollow steel circles are pressed
and warped by the flanks of the doomed,
whose greasy sides have jostled grey
tubes into artistic singularity. Despite all
foreshadowing, the space is charmed,
scent full of musky pasture, ripened straw.

Off the walls and roof waves
soldiers' voices ricochet

Suddenly, contact. They soar.
All that is solid melts
into a spontaneous balletic lift -
all is creamy, foamy, floaty blur
and dust and chaff and selling

57

tags shrink to nought.

Off the walls and roof waves
soldiers' voices ricochet

Sunbeam spotlights blast their Icarus smiles,
swipe their cheeks, poke closed eyes.
A muss of spun gold slips through dry
fingers; his elbows pinch in, scuff her thighs.
Knocked out of sync, her feet, one by
one, bounce the dust off the concrete steps.

The children shriek, push past and run outside.

Annisa Suliman recently completed a PhD which explored Victorian periodicals. A retired university lecturer, she previously spent 20 years as a media professional. Prizewinning poems include: Ice-Etching (Unbound Press, 2010); Fetish (2nd prize, Ilkley Literature Festival, 2009; and Curlyhead (shortlisted, York Open Poetry Competition, 1999).

Trev Wainwright

A Yorkshireman

Tha can tell a Yorkshireman it sez like as such
But one thing tha can't, tha can't tell him much
Instead of shut the door, it's put t' wood in t'oil
When tha's doin thi best he'll not say summat nasty
He'll say gerron wi thi an gi it some pasty
And if it's been a while since his house you've entered in
He'll greet you with "Eh up, nar then where's tha bin?"
Instead of make it's meck, instead of break its breck
An when it all goes wrong he'll sat flippin' eck
So for woke its wock'n and for broke its brock'n
If you want to know anything, also known as owt
He'll give advice for free sayin' "Ah'll tell thee that fer nowt"
And when he finds life's beyond a joke.
He'll say "There's nowt as queer as folk"
If instead of how are you, you ask how you diddlin'?
He'll say 'appen Ah'm fair to middlin'
Aye tha can tell a Yorkshireman it sez like as such
But one thing tha can't, tha can't tell him much

Inspired by a Yorkshire saying on a tee shirt, and given to Skipton Museum where the tee short as bought from, to raise funds, it has proved very popular with visitors.

Trev, an international poet, born in Wakefield based in Castleford, has a pride in is Yorkshire heritage he featured on Radio 4 as a Dialect Poet in 2019. Often performs wearing Yorkshire tops and a baseball hat. He also loves adapting songs and bible stories and setting them in Yorkshire. Well known in Texas, often referred to there as Yorkshire's Poetry Ambassador.

Lizi Walker

She was free

As she stepped out of the self contained bubble that she had kept
herself in for most of her life
She gasped as the air hit the back of her throat and the breeze blew
across her face
She was free
She was finally free
As she stumbled out into pastures new
The road ahead unfamiliar and daunting
Butterflies in her tummy
Her head spinning with thoughts of what lie ahead
New adventures
New possibilities
Places she had never been
People she had never met
Things she had never done
A world that she had never allowed herself to feel or experience
Fear and anxiety had kept her trapped in her comfort zone
Existing instead of living
Her body trembled with fear and excitement
Fear of not knowing where this path would lead her too
Would she be safe
Could she do this
Excitement of what lie ahead
An inner knowing that she was been divinely guided

She had finally allowed herself to step out onto the path of freedom
and endless possibilities
She was free
She was no longer going to allow fear and anxiety to keep her stuck
She was going to walk this path no matter what it took
She was going to walk it with faith
She was going to walk with courage
She was going to walk it with pride
With the trust that no matter where it took her
It would always lead her to where she needed to be
She was free and she was unstoppable

Elizabeth Walker lives in a small quite village in North Yorkshire
which she shares with her daughter and their pets. She enjoys walks
in the countryside, writing poetry along with reading and researching
for the truth.

Lindsay Walter

The sounds of the Terrace

At night,
drunks.
Night birds.
Soughing trees.
A buzzing streetlight,
silver midges lured and circling.
The seldom sounds of darkness
float, pavements
stretched like sandbars,
wet tarmac water-
smooth and black. Ghosts
hang in the hedges
with the raindrops
and the litter.

In the morning
sound rises. Wells
like a spring through sand, brims,
spills.
Footsteps slap. Words
splash and whirlpool.
He said and *she said* and *they say...* bubble
and float *pop!*
into oblivion.
Cars surge.

Through the flood, blaring,
a siren tsunamis.
Silence fishtails
on a bike.

Lindsay has lived in many different places, from Bradford to-
Bourne- mouth, Switzerland to Malta, but she was born and brought
up in a village in a valley in North Yorkshire. There was a lime tree
outside her bedroom window, a beck ran past the garden, owls
called from the woods at midnight.

Debbie Watson

Diving

Her phone call comes
  at just past four
    when I'm rushing out the door
      to catch the post.
She floods into my life
  out of synch-after an absence,
    needing to wash up on my shore.
  Capsized by old rock rubbles
    she never swims free from.

The others, too,
    were racked up-wrecked,
      in the blue, drowning-
        the heavy folk, thrashing madly in the waves.
      They did not brave
        the fathoms below,
          to work free what anchors them.
            I did what I could to get them to try,
            having dived, myself long ago.
          I know that the deep
        is the place to survive,
      when tsunamis crash down from behind.

Deborah Watson, from York, began writing forty years ago from expressive need to make sense of her inner process. Her writings later developed into accessible, eclectic styles to include her observations and social comment on, life, nature and the human condition -from the mundane to the mystical.

Steve Williams

Behind the Scenes

These are the men from behind the scenes,
Spilling from vans in paint-pocked jeans.
These are the lads from the college, the tech;
The back-pocket trainees rejecting the cheque.

The blokes with the 'eh up', the 'no problem love';
The radio thumping three floors up above.
The guys with the panels, the pliers, the pins;
The quick cup of tea before grafting begins.

This is the crowd that can make it all happen:
The sawing, the slicing, the screwing, the snapping;
The gouging, the gauging, the grinding, the grout;
The having it done while the family's out.

These are the lads watching City, United;
That weigh up our wrongs and get them alrighted.
These are the boys with the gossip, the tales;
These are the hammers that knock in the nails.

These are the kids with the KitKats and Coke,
The banter, the Fanta, the stories, the jokes.
The guys that can handle the stuff we can't do.
These are the fixers. The concrete. The glue.

Steve Williams is an English teacher by day and a quirky northern poet whenever he can find the time. He writes comedy poems (hopefully) and verse that bends to the far-off rolling hills of nostalgia. He has been Poet in Residence at BBC Radio York and he has a strong portfolio of commissions, from weddings to York City FC.

Amie-May Wilson

Unacquainted love

I tried everything.
I tried the blaming,
Him or me or both.
I tried the picking,
Was it this or that.
I tried optimism,
You are not unlovable.

I now have it figured.
He was the moon whilst I was the sun.
Very compatible,
Yet so out of reach.
Wishing amongst the stars,
For a different galaxy,
One that favoured us more.

One that would defy all,
Just so we could be close.

Though we can't dream for the impossible,
It's more complicated than our minds like to believe.
The moon moved placidly around the sun,
Whilst the sun tried to radiate rays of warmth his way.
The sun deserved the same love in return,
but the moon is stuck in his ways.

And I trust when the moon cries,
This too isn't the outcome he wanted.
But when he isn't glowing as bright,
There was no other option that night.

He let her go,
Watched her from afar.
The sun and the moon,
Wished upon different stars.

Unacquainted Love by Amie-May Wilson, a 20 year old poet, describes a type of love that was never quite fulfilled, but not quite dismissed. It is metaphorically bittersweet, entailing imagery of the sun and the moon.

Tamara Wilson

Merelots

The Monday after Easter
is the day of the dead.
A day to unearth, a day to greet
all your past selves, your hidden pains.
One face at a time they will appear
whilst you hold your hushed, one-man vigil
Most faces are as nameless as you now
most places frozen and still.

Merelots (Western Armenian): A day of prayer and remembrance dedicated to the commemoration of the departed in the Armenian Apostolic Church, akin to All Souls' Day in Western Christianity.

Dr Tamara Wilson is a poet, academic and Honorary Research Fellow at the University of Roehampton, London. Alongside the Armenian and Greek heritage of modern-day Turkey, she is interested in the exploration of identity and memory through hybrid literary and non-literary forms. Currently she is working on the adaptation of her verse novel into a stage production.

Tom Wilson

Ward 36 blues

Yeah I know
I know what its like
On ward 35
Waking up flustered and paranoid
As they are zipping up some bloke in a body bag
Like a military operation
A squadron of nurses march in
And he is erased from memory
Taken to ward 36
There is no ward 36
It's actually the morgue
When you have to wriggle around
Showing em you aint dead yet
As they use you as canella target practice
Moody nurses
Drained by tory scum
Demoralised and spent
The cold toilets
The smell of the dude in the next bed
Its always pungent fresh hot piss
like a finale physical indictment
The food was cold and made of throbbing felt
I was in the dimly lit side ward
Like being on remand from death
but he kept strolling passed my door

and grinning in, did death
i waited there, fermenting
Till they cleared my test
But it came back positive
then, all belongings are hastily packed
They shoved me in the bleak ward
With the rotted stories and the dying dreams
Spinning and gyrating in fear
all moonless night long
The light changes
from low to stark
You hear Van Morrison strains from outside
As the nurses pile back in
with renewed energy and venomous determination
Loaded with perfume so pungent that it makes your eyes bleed
You don't know if it's dawn or dust
It makes no difference
no tv unless you pay to be patronised
no news papers allowed
Your staying in that bed
Tablets and water are rammed at you
Giddy nurses and sterile Doctors
Patrol the newly mopped floors
It beats waking up in ICU
Waking up in ICU
Coming round from a surreal train wreck
As a terrified Asian chap was climbing up the wall to try and escape
I had more wires and tubes sticking out of me
Than a trendy bang and olufsen hi fi system

I just had to lie still
Like a fragile installation
On show at the tate....

Tom Wilson was born in Salford in 1958. He has been writing since 1975. He lives in North Yorkshire where he also paints and Directs theatre. He has written plays, songs, comedy routines and short films. He endeavours to write everyday, sometimes it's just rough notes or the skeleton of a future piece. Poetry is his main speaking, honest and vulnerable yet forthright voice and he feels his poems are a kind of an abstract diary of his emotional up's downs and otherwise life. Poetry seems to be his ink with which he captures his memories, anxieties, wounded dreams, tenuous victories and feelings with.

Alison Young

Ripples

Ripples…
Dancing in the water
Toying with the day,
Engaged in play.
A kaleidoscope of colours
Erupting on the surface
As the honest sun beats down;
Caressing my frown.
Life's a be-ach
Then you die,
Existing in places
Beyond the why.
Just leaving behind
Sweet traces of life,
Like…Ripples.

Alison Young is a Yorkshire creative. She works as a performer; director and writer. Alison has a degree in Psychology (BSc) and is a qualified Yoga instructor. Writing poetry is a form of expression that she has used as a therapeutic tool since childhood; and she loves sharing the power of how words can change and shape our worlds.

About the Editor

James P. Wagner (Ishwa) is an editor, publisher, award-winning fiction writer, essayist, historian, performance poet, and alum twice over (BA & MALS) of Dowling College. He is the publisher for Local Gems Poetry Press and the Senior Founder and President of the Bards Initiative. He is also the founder and Grand Laureate of Bards Against Hunger, a series of poetry readings and anthologies dedicated to gathering food for local pantries that operates in over a dozen states. His most recent individual collection of poetry is *Everyday Alchemy*. He was the Long Island, NY National Beat Poet Laureate from 2017-2019. He was the Walt Whitman Bicentennial Convention Chairman and teaches poetry workshops at the Walt Whitman Birthplace State Historic Site. James has edited over 100 poetry anthologies and hosted book launch events up and down the East Coast. He was named the National Beat Poet Laureate of the United States from 2020-2021. He is the owner/operator of The Dog-Eared Bard's Book Shop in East Northport, NY.

Made in the USA
Monee, IL
15 May 2022

96465152R00046